BREAKING BARRIERS

The Story of Jackie Robinson

S0-BNQ-402

BY MICHAEL BURGAN

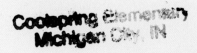

Coolspring Elementary
Michigan City, IN

Consultant:
Richard Bell, PhD
Associate Professor of History
University of Maryland, College Park

CAPSTONE PRESS
a capstone imprint
Coolspring Media Center

Tangled History is published by Capstone Press,
1710 Roe Crest Drive, North Mankato, Minnesota 56003
www.mycapstone.com

Library of Congress Cataloging-in-Publication data is available on the Library of
Congress website.

978-1-5157-7932-2 (library binding)
978-1-5157-7963-6 (paperback)
978-1-5157-7967-4 (eBook PDF)

Editorial Credits
Adrian Vigliano, editor; Bobbie Nuytten, designer; Svetlana Zhurkin, media
researcher; Katy LaVigne, production specialist

Photo Credits
AP Photo: John J. Lent, 50; Getty Images: © 2017 NBCUniversal/NBC, 103, Archive
Photos, 27, Bettmann, 13, 30, 63, 64, 73, 83, 97, 99, Carnegie Museum of Art/Teenie
Harris Archive/Charles "Teenie" Harris, 8, CBS Photo Archive, 78-79, Gado/Afro
American Newspapers, 88, IH Images/Irving Haberman, 86, 101, Sporting News,
67, Sports Studio Photos/International News Photography, 38, The LIFE Picture
Collection/J.R. Eyerman, 45, Transcendental Graphics/Mark Rucker, 4, 92; Granger,
NYC, 55; Newscom: akg-images, 74, Everett Collection, 15, 23, Picture History, 7;
Science Source, cover; Shutterstock: Ksenia Krylova, 105

Printed and bound in the United States of America.
010829S18

TABLE OF CONTENTS

Moses Fleetwood Walker (top right) played with the Syracuse Stars of the International League from 1888 to 1889.

FOREWORD

In 1945 two professional baseball leagues prepared to start their seasons. The better known of the two was Major League Baseball, which had 16 teams across the Northeast and Midwest. Its players, all white, made good salaries and played in large, well-maintained ballparks. Some of the Major League cities also had teams from the Negro Leagues. With a few exceptions, the black players on those teams struggled to earn a living.

In the early days of professional baseball, blacks and whites had sometimes played together. Moses Fleetwood Walker is often considered the first African-American to play in a professional league. He played for several teams including the Toledo Blue Stockings of the American Association during the 1884 season. But soon after that the pro teams set up what was called the color line. The color line was a form of segregation and meant that black players could no longer play with whites in Major League Baseball. White players with racist attitudes simply refused to play with — or even against — African-Americans. With the best teams and the highest salaries, Major League teams remained the desired goal for every ballplayer. But the color line ensured that even the best black players had no hope of making these teams.

During the 1930s and early 1940s, a small number of Americans, some of them black sportswriters, called for integrated baseball. World War II (1939–1945) boosted the efforts of people who wanted to see the color line broken.

The United States fought to defeat leaders in Germany, Italy, and Japan who did not believe in democracy or equality. Blacks and others argued that if inequality and lack of freedom were wrong elsewhere, they were wrong in the United States too. Black American military personnel were facing the same risks as whites in battle, but they were not treated equally at home.

One black American who served in the military during the war was Jackie Robinson. He had been a star athlete in four sports while in high school and at the University of California at Los Angeles (UCLA). Many people believed Robinson was skilled enough to play baseball in the Majors. In 1945 he got his chance to prove it.

The 1932 Pittsburgh Crawfords. The Crawfords of
the 1930s are still considered one of the best Negro
League teams ever assembled.

1945

1

Wendell Smith

Wendell Smith

Boston, Massachusetts, April 16, 1945

Wendell Smith walked into Boston's Fenway Park, home of the Red Sox. As a sports reporter, he had spent time in many ballparks. But this visit was different.

Smith entered Fenway Park with three ballplayers from the Negro Leagues by his side. The players were scheduled to try out for the Red Sox and perhaps play for them in the future. One player was Marvin "Hitter" Williams, an infielder with the Philadelphia Stars. The second was outfielder Sam Jethroe of the Cleveland Buckeyes, known as "the Jet" because of his speed. The third player was Jackie Robinson, a shortstop for the Kansas City Monarchs.

Smith's efforts to get black players a tryout with the Red Sox had some history. In 1944 Boston city councilman Isadore Muchnick wrote to the Red Sox insisting that the team let black players try out. If not, Muchnick promised to deny the Red Sox the special permission they needed to play Sunday games in Boston. Red Sox general manager Eddie Collins responded that no African-Americans wanted to play for the club. Collins' claim wasn't surprising. Major League team owners and managers typically insisted that baseball's color line didn't even exist.

When Smith heard about Collins' response, he wrote Muchnick. He said he could find plenty of black ballplayers eager to play for the Red Sox.

For Smith, breaking the color line was personal. In his high school days in the early 1930s, he had been a star pitcher. But he had known he would never be recruited by a Major League team because he was black. After joining the *Pittsburgh Courier,* a newspaper for African-Americans, he made it his mission to break baseball's color line.

Smith didn't necessarily think the three players with him today were the best players in the Negro Leagues. But he thought Robinson in particular had qualities that would be important if a Major League team wanted to sign him. Robinson had not actively played baseball for several years because of his time in the military. But he had played on integrated teams before. Smith suspected that Robinson knew the kind of racism he would face and would be able to deal with it. But he would also stand up for himself when he needed to.

Muchnick and several Red Sox officials watched the three black ballplayers that day. Collins was nowhere to be seen. As the tryouts went on, Robinson's performance stood out. At the plate, he hit several home runs over Fenway's famous "Green Monster" wall in left field. Impressive as Robinson's performance was, Smith had to wonder if the Red Sox would seriously consider signing a black player. He suspected there would be more work to do to help a black player break baseball's color line.

Branch Rickey

Brooklyn, New York, May 1945

The baseball season was underway when Branch Rickey met with Wendell Smith. Rickey was the president and part owner of the Major League Brooklyn Dodgers. He had just told the press that he wanted to form a new, all-black team called the Brooklyn Brown Dodgers.

The team would play in a new league and use Ebbets Field, the Dodgers' home park.

Rickey knew of Smith's interest in integrating baseball and the Boston tryout. In his office Rickey asked, "Were there any players in your group really good enough to make the Majors?"

"There was one player who could make good in any league," Smith replied. "Jackie Robinson."

"Jackie Robinson!" Rickey said. "I knew he was an All-American football player … but I didn't know he played baseball."

Rickey was interested in what Smith had to say about Robinson's skills on the field and his personality off of it. Rickey didn't tell Smith, but in recent years he'd begun considering signing a black player to the Brooklyn Dodgers. The team had never won a World Series. Rickey knew that some of the best players in the Negro Leagues could certainly help the Dodgers pursue a championship. But Rickey also saw breaking the color barrier as the right thing to do. And he had the support of the Dodgers' other owners.

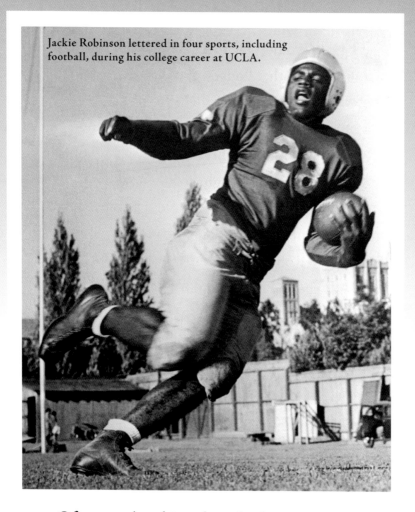

Jackie Robinson lettered in four sports, including football, during his college career at UCLA.

Of course, breaking the color line was sure to generate a lot of criticism from other Major League team owners. It would also upset some fans and players with racist attitudes.

Rickey was sure the worst reactions would be in the South. The so-called Jim Crow laws segregating blacks and whites seemed to be stronger than ever in Southern states.

Rickey followed up by talking to many people who had known Robinson throughout his life. He learned that Robinson had faced a military court-martial in 1944 after pushing back against racist treatment. The incident happened while Robinson was riding on a bus back to his army base in Fort Hood, Texas. After riding for a few blocks, the white driver abruptly ordered Robinson to move to the back of the bus. Robinson refused, leading to his arrest by military police. When military officials questioned him later, Robinson said he felt he had not been respected as an officer (he was a lieutenant). He had gotten angry, especially when an officer called him by a racial slur. But Robinson just wanted to be treated fairly. He was found not guilty at the court-martial and later received an honorable discharge.

Jackie Robinson played with the Kansas City
Monarchs of the Negro Leagues in 1945.

Rickey kept talking to people and learning more about Robinson. It seemed clear that he would stand up for himself, as he had in the military. Robinson seemed to have the courage to do what was right. But he also appeared to be someone who could keep his cool if he were attacked. Rickey began to feel that Robinson could be the right man to crack the color line.

Clyde Sukeforth

Brooklyn, New York, August 1945

Clyde Sukeforth sat in Branch Rickey's office. Sukeforth worked for the Brooklyn Dodgers as a scout. He traveled around the country to find players who might be good enough to play in the Major Leagues. For about the past year, part of Sukeforth's job was to attend Negro League games and look for talented players. His next trip was to Chicago. There he would watch a Negro League game between the Chicago American Giants and the Kansas City Monarchs.

"I want you to see that fellow Robinson on Kansas City," Rickey told Sukeforth. "Tell him who sent you. Tell him I want to know if he's got a shortstop's arm."

If Sukeforth liked what he saw, he knew Rickey would want to see Robinson play in person. But Sukeforth had a sense that Rickey was not just interested in signing Robinson to the Brown Dodgers.

On August 24 Sukeforth sat in the stands for the first game between the Monarchs and the American Giants. He spotted Robinson on the field. Sukeforth made his way toward the field to tell Robinson about Rickey's interest in him.

"Why is he interested in me?" Robinson asked.

"That is a good question," Sukeforth replied. "And I wish I had the answer for you. But I don't."

Robinson explained that he had injured his shoulder and wouldn't be playing for about a week. Sukeforth told Robinson he wanted to talk to him again after the game. He told the player to meet him at his hotel. Robinson agreed.

Jackie Robinson

Jackie Robinson arrived in Clyde Sukeforth's hotel room ready to press the scout for more information. He got right to it.

"Why is Branch Rickey interested in me and my arm?" Robinson asked. After a moment he added, "You can't blame me for being curious, can you?"

Sukeforth replied, "I can't blame you, because I'm just as curious as you."

Robinson was curious, but also cautious. After the tryout in Boston, he doubted that any Major League team really wanted to sign a black player.

Sukeforth began talking about the Brooklyn Brown Dodgers. He said it was possible that Rickey wanted Robinson to be on that team. But Sukeforth also hinted that Rickey might be thinking about something else for Robinson.

Then Sukeforth said that if Robinson couldn't come to Brooklyn, Rickey was prepared to come out and meet him. Robinson hadn't expected that. He was impressed.

Robinson knew he had been playing well for the Monarchs, but he didn't like life in the Negro Leagues. The team traveled long distances by bus and had to stay in cheap hotels that only accepted black guests. The rooms were usually dirty and the players sometimes found the bathrooms unusable. Things were frustrating on the playing field too. Many umpires were not skilled and the teams didn't keep accurate records.

Sukeforth said he was headed to Toledo, Ohio, next. Robinson agreed to meet him there, and then go with him to Brooklyn.

I have nothing to lose, he thought.

With Clyde Sukeforth by his side, Jackie Robinson walked into Branch Rickey's office. After shaking hands, Rickey startled Robinson with his first question.

"You got a girl?" the Dodgers' president asked.

"I don't know," Robinson said.

"What do you mean, you don't know?" Rickey asked.

"I have a girl, but things between us have been a little rough lately," Robinson said. "But we're engaged and we want to get married."

Rickey seemed to like that. "When we get through today you may want to call her up," he said. "Because there are times when a man needs a woman by his side."

Robinson felt his heart beat faster. He thought Rickey had invited him to Brooklyn to play for the Brown Dodgers. Now he wasn't sure.

"I've sent for you because I'm interested in you for the Brooklyn Dodgers," Rickey said. "I think you can play in the Major Leagues."

Robinson sat speechless.

Rickey continued, "You think you can play for Montreal?"

Robinson knew the Montreal Royals were the Dodgers' top farm club. He took a deep breath and said, "Yes."

Rickey explained that he had been searching for a while to find the right player to break the color line. "I know you're a good ballplayer," he said. "But what I'm looking for is more than a good player. I'm looking for a man that will take insults, take abuse — and not fight back!"

Rickey described the abuse Robinson would have to endure. Fans and other players would hurl racial slurs at him, and some players might even try to injure him. Pitchers might throw at his head and runners might slide into base with their sharp spikes aimed at Robinson's legs.

On the road, he would face all the racism that fed the Jim Crow laws and attitudes that kept blacks segregated from whites. Rickey wanted to know if Robinson could keep his cool despite all that.

Robinson thought about times in his life when he had faced prejudice. His first impulse was always to stand up for himself, even fight back, if necessary.

"Are you looking for a Negro who is afraid to fight back?" he asked.

Rickey answered hotly, "Robinson, I'm looking for a ballplayer with guts enough *not* to fight back."

Rickey asked again if Robinson still wanted to sign with the Brooklyn Dodgers. "Certainly," Robinson replied.

Roy Campanella

After the Negro Leagues season ended, Roy Campanella joined other ballplayers on a brief New York vacation. From there, they would head off to play winter baseball in places such as Venezuela. Campanella was a catcher. He was only 23, but he had been a Negro Leagues star for several years. In the Woodside Hotel in Harlem, New York, Campanella saw Jackie Robinson.

Roy Campanella (left) began playing baseball professionally when he was just 15.

They had only played against each other twice that season, but now they'd met to talk and play cards.

As they played, Robinson asked about Campanella's recent visit to Branch Rickey's office. "Did Mr. Rickey tell you that he wanted you for the Brown Dodgers?" Robinson asked.

Campanella said no, but he had assumed that was why Rickey had wanted to see him. "What about you? Did you sign?" Campanella asked.

"Yes," Robinson said. "But not to play for the Brown Dodgers. I'm going to play for Montreal."

Campanella heard the excitement in Robinson's voice.

"Do you realize what this means, Campy?" Robinson asked. "It's the end of Jim Crow in baseball."

Shocked at what he heard, Campanella kept puffing on a cigar that was no longer lit. He saw the happiness that filled Robinson's face, and the two men grinned at each other. Campanella was happy too. He wondered if Rickey had plans to have him join Robinson.

Robinson told Campanella not to tell anyone about his signing a contract because the news was still a secret. The next day, Robinson was going to Montreal to announce publicly that he was going to play for the Royals. But he had needed to tell someone his good news.

As Robinson got up to leave, Campanella put his hand on his friend's shoulder. "I'm glad for you, Jackie, real glad, "he said. "You're a good ballplayer, you'll make it. I've played with white teams, lots of them — with them and against them. They're men, just like us. There's nothing to worry about."

"I hope so," Robinson said. "I sure hope so."

Jackie Robinson

Jackie Robinson walked into the offices of the Montreal Royals and saw about two dozen journalists waiting. With Robinson were two team officials and Branch Rickey Jr., Branch Rickey's son, known as "The Twig." He headed up the Dodgers' system of farm teams.

As Robinson looked out at the room filled with white journalists, he tried to remain cool and calm. But he felt nervous as he never had before. He listened as Hector Racine, president of the Royals, announced that the team had signed Robinson.

Jackie Robinson broke the minor league color line when he signed with the Montreal Royals in 1945.

The room fell silent for a moment, as the journalists realized what they had just heard. Then it hit them — the Dodgers were breaking baseball's color line! Cameras began flashing as reporters shouted questions.

Racine explained that the decision to sign Robinson was based on both his talents and on fairness. He recalled how black soldiers had fought and died next to white soldiers in the war. He said black players had earned the right to compete with whites on the ball field.

Then it was Robinson's turn to speak. He knew he had to choose his words carefully. What he said would be reported across both Canada and the United States. He didn't want to say the wrong thing. That might cost him the support of some sportswriters and baseball fans before he had even put on a Royals uniform. He knew he was taking part in a "racial experiment." This was not just about his playing in the Major Leagues. He was taking a step for equality and justice for all blacks.

Speaking calmly, Robinson said, "Of course, I can't begin to tell you how happy I am … I can only say I'll do my very best to come through in every manner."

Robinson read the newspapers to learn about the reactions of baseball players and team owners. Some players, current and former — and especially those from the South — opposed integrating baseball. Others said it was fine with them if Robinson played well enough in Montreal to earn his way to the Dodgers.

About 10 days after his meeting with the Montreal press, Robinson spoke to Michael Carter of the *Baltimore Afro-American*. The *Afro-American* was a newspaper for black readers. Robinson talked about the future. He felt his success would make it easier for young black athletes to compete with whites. On and off the field, Robinson knew, white eyes would be watching how he acted.

"I feel that if I flop, or conduct myself badly … that I'll set the advancement of blacks back a hundred years," he told Carter.

Then Robinson headed off to Venezuela to play winter baseball. His chance to help advance the position of blacks everywhere would wait until next spring.

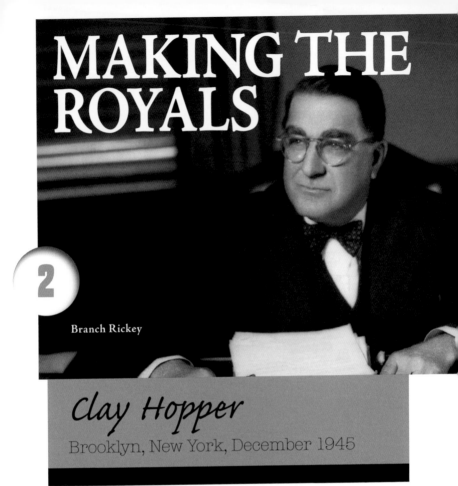

MAKING THE ROYALS

2

Branch Rickey

Clay Hopper

Brooklyn, New York, December 1945

Clay Hopper sat opposite Branch Rickey in the president's office. He wasn't sure why his boss wanted to see him. Rickey had given Hopper his first job as a minor league baseball manager in 1929. When Rickey took over the Dodgers, he hired Hopper

to manage Brooklyn's farm team in Mobile, Alabama. The recently completed 1945 season had been Hopper's first managing the Mobile Bears.

Hopper, a native Mississippian, planned to work in the cotton business in his home state during the off-season. But now he found himself in Brooklyn, waiting to hear why Rickey had called him in.

"I have good news," Rickey told Hopper. "I want you to manage the Montreal Royals."

This was good news. Montreal was the Dodgers' top farm team, just one step below the Majors.

"And I want you to know," Rickey continued, "that at least one player on the team will be a Negro."

That information didn't stun Hopper. He, like everyone in baseball, knew that the Dodgers had signed Jackie Robinson. But now he realized that the promotion wasn't so good after all. Rickey wanted him, a Southerner, to manage a black player.

"Please don't do this to me," Hopper said. "I'm white and I've lived in Mississippi all my life. If you're going to do this, you're going to force me to move my family and home out of Mississippi."

But Rickey would not back down. He said, "You manage this fellow the way I want him managed, and you figure out the way I want him managed."

"Yes, Mr. Rickey," Hopper said.

"Clay, this is the greatest opportunity of your life," Rickey said encouragingly. "Managing Robinson, winning with him, can turn out to be a great accomplishment for you. I believe you are up to it."

Growing up in the South, Hopper had been taught that black people and white people were not equal. He even knew those who thought black people weren't human at all. But now, if he wanted to stay with the Dodgers, he had to put aside his old attitudes and beliefs. His father would probably sooner have killed him than see his son managing a black baseball player. But his father was dead.

Hopper finally agreed to take the job with Montreal. He would figure out a way to manage Jackie Robinson.

Rachel Robinson
Los Angeles, California, February 28, 1946

Rachel Robinson stood in the Los Angeles airport terminal, ready to fly to Florida with her new husband. She and Jack had gotten married in Los Angeles a little more than two weeks ago. She always called him Jack, just like his family did. Rachel had been in nursing school while Jack served in the military and started his baseball career. Now, she had her degree, and she felt sure that they were starting a long and wonderful life together.

Before they boarded the plane, Jack's mother, Mallie, handed the couple a box.

"What's this?" Jack asked.

Mrs. Robinson explained that it held fried chicken and hard-boiled eggs.

"I just thought something might happen and I didn't want you starving to death," she said.

Rachel had no intention of eating the food on the way. She imagined white people making fun of them for eating the food Mrs. Robinson gave them. She knew people with racist beliefs thought black people turned their trips into rowdy picnics by bringing their own food. But not wanting to be rude, Rachel and Jack took the box before boarding their plane.

The Robinsons flew first to New Orleans. Growing up in California, Rachel had never experienced the legal segregation of the South. Still, she had experienced plenty of racism in California. But now, for the first time ever, Rachel saw for herself the reality of the South under Jim Crow. Signs marked drinking fountains and restrooms as being for "white" or "colored" people. Rachel ignored one sign and used a "white" bathroom. She did it intentionally, to show her resistance to the segregation around her. People stared at her, but they left her alone.

Meanwhile, the Robinsons had been bumped from their scheduled flight to Florida. Then they were bumped from another flight. Not knowing when they would finally leave, Jack went to find food. When he came back, Rachel sensed he was ready to explode with anger.

"They won't serve us in the restaurant here," he told Rachel. "We can get sandwiches at one place — if we don't eat the food there."

Rachel felt her own anger rise up. She was not used to be treating as a second-class citizen. "I won't eat that way," she said.

Realizing they would not leave anytime soon, they went to wait at a nearby hotel that served black people. Walking into the hotel room, Rachel was appalled at how dirty and dingy it was. There were cobwebs everywhere.

They took out the box of food that Mrs. Robinson had given them. Mallie must have known what Jack and Rachel might face as they traveled through the South. Rachel now understood why her mother-in-law had prepared the food for them.

The next day, the couple finally boarded a plane to Florida. After landing in Pensacola, Florida, to refuel, the Robinsons were told they were being bumped again. Jack went to argue with the airline workers. As he walked back to Rachel she could see the anger that filled him. It seemed like a rage he could barely contain. He told her that the airline employees insisted they had no seats for the Robinsons. A white couple took the seats the Robinsons had just left. Rachel was afraid that Jackie might hit someone, and their dreams of his successful future in baseball would disappear.

The couple finally caught a bus that took them to Daytona Beach, Florida. On the ride, Rachel cried quietly, so Jackie wouldn't see how upset she was. She was crying for him, knowing how helpless he felt as they faced the discrimination all around them.

Jackie Robinson

Jackie Robinson walked toward the clubhouse at the park in Sanford, Florida, where the Royals were beginning spring training. Managers and team officials used spring training to decide if a player would be assigned to a team in the organization. The best players would be on the Dodgers or a top farm team such as the Royals when the season started. Although Rickey wanted Robinson on the Royals, there was no guarantee he would make the team.

Johnny Wright, a pitcher, walked next to Robinson. Johnny was another black player trying to make the Majors. As they got closer to the field, Robinson could feel the stares of the white players already out there.

In the clubhouse, Robinson put on his uniform and got ready to join the other players. "Well," he said, "this is it."

Robinson and Wright headed out of the clubhouse together. They were met by reporters, who quickly fired off questions. One asked Robinson what he would do if a pitcher tried to hit him with a pitch.

"The same thing everybody else does — duck!" Robinson said, smiling.

After a few more questions, Robinson and Wright went over to meet their new manager. Robinson knew that Clay Hopper was a Southerner, but he wasn't sure how Hopper felt

Johnny Wright (center left) and Jackie Robinson (center right) at spring training in Florida, 1946.

about integrated baseball. As they got closer, Robinson was relieved to see Hopper offer his hand to shake. Hopper's speech was sharp and quick, but he talked pleasantly to both men before offering some pitching advice to Wright.

The day went smoothly for Robinson. When practice ended, he and Wright headed to the house of Viola and David Brock. The Brocks were a black couple who had opened up their home to the players.

The ballplayers talked about their day. They told Mr. Brock that they were pleasantly surprised that things had gone so well.

"You'll find good people everywhere you go," Mr. Brock said. "Yes sir, even here in Florida."

Wendell Smith

Sanford, Florida, March 5, 1946

Wendell Smith and Billy Rowe spent the second day of spring training at the Brock home, waiting for Robinson. Rowe was a photographer for Smith's paper, the *Pittsburgh Courier*. Branch Rickey had hired them to stay with Robinson during spring training. He wanted them to help Robinson adjust to life in a Jim Crow state. As they sat on the porch, a white man approached them.

"The folks here in Sanford sent me here to give you a message. We want you to get out of town," the man said, adding a racial slur. "You'd all better be out of here by nightfall, or there will be trouble."

Smith called Branch Rickey and asked him what to do. He told Smith to take Robinson and Wright to Daytona Beach as soon as possible.

When Robinson and Wright got back to the house, they joined the others for dinner. Usually, Smith was quick to joke with the players, but this evening he was quiet. When dinner was over, Rowe said he was going to get gas for the car.

"We should be able to get out of here in 15 or 20 minutes," Smith said.

Robinson asked if the two journalists were leaving them.

"No." Smith said. "We're all going to Daytona."

Robinson heard Wendell Smith get on the phone to Branch Rickey. He said they would be ready to leave soon. Robinson didn't understand why they were all heading back to Daytona Beach. Was Rickey ending his effort to integrate baseball? Why would he, especially when the first two days of spring training had gone so well? The questions racing through his mind turned to anger as he packed his bags and got into Rowe's car.

The four men sat silently as Rowe drove toward Daytona Beach. At a stoplight, they saw a group of white men standing on the corner.

"How can they call themselves Americans?" Rowe asked, looking at the white men.

"They're as rotten as they come," Smith said.

Robinson didn't understand these comments. He had been treated well by the locals so far. "They haven't done anything to us," he said.

"They're nice people as far as I'm concerned," Wright agreed.

Smith turned around to face Robinson and Wright in the back seat. "Look, we didn't want to tell you guys because we didn't want to upset you," he said. "We want you to make this ball club. But … we're leaving this town because we were told to get out. They won't stand for Negro ballplayers on the same field as whites!"

Robinson felt embarrassment wash over him. Maybe trying to help integrate baseball had been a mistake. But how would getting out of Sanford help, he wondered. Surely he and Wright would face the same racism in Daytona Beach. Then he thought about the millions of black Americans who were counting on him. He knew he would have to stay with the team and try his best. This wasn't over yet.

Rachel Robinson

Rachel Robinson soon joined Jack in Daytona Beach. As she learned about the racism Jack experienced, Rachel wished she could protect him. But she knew she couldn't. All she could do was listen to his anger and frustration, which grew as he struggled to play his best. She went to the practices and saw Clay Hopper and Branch Rickey move him from one position to another. They were trying to see where he could best help the Royals. She watched him have trouble hitting the pitching he faced. When he hurt his throwing arm, she put ice packs on his body to try to help him heal. On many nights, she watched him toss in bed, unable to sleep.

Rachel and Jack had known each other for five years, and their experience in Florida continued drawing them even closer together.

But Rachel kept one secret. She learned that she was pregnant. She decided to wait to tell Jack, so he wouldn't have one more thing to think about.

Jackie Robinson

Daytona Beach, Florida, March 1946

As March went on, Jackie Robinson began to feel more comfortable. In one exhibition game, he noticed white fans clapping for him when he came to the plate. And for the most part, his white teammates accepted him. Robinson, though, mostly kept to himself, determined to improve his play and make the team.

The people in Daytona Beach did not seem as prejudiced as some in Florida. But when the Royals traveled to Jacksonville, Florida, local officials refused to allow the integrated team on the field. As Robinson and the other players got off their bus, they could see the gates to the field were locked. Robinson felt bad. He couldn't help but feel responsible for the cancellation.

But it was good to see that so many fans had come to the park. He wondered if they had come to see him play.

In early April, as spring training was winding down, the Royals went to Sanford to play a game. Jackie remembered the fast exit he and Johnny Wright had made just a month before. He wondered how this game would turn out.

This sign, used in *The Jackie Robinson Story* film, dramatized the cancelled Royals game.

Clay Hopper

Sanford, Florida, April 7, 1946

Clay Hopper decided to put Jackie Robinson at second base for the Royals' game in Sanford. In the second inning, Hopper watched Robinson hit a single. A few pitches later, he stole second base. Hopper thought back to the attitudes he'd had about black people before managing an integrated team. Slowly, he was coming to see that he had been too harsh. He had been wrong to think that Robinson or other blacks might not even be human.

Now Robinson used his great speed to score from second on a teammate's hit. Just then, Hopper noticed a police officer walking onto the field. As Robinson got up after sliding across home plate, the officer grabbed him by the collar. After a moment, the officer released him. Hopper left the dugout to talk to the cop.

"What's wrong?" Hopper asked. "He didn't do anything wrong, did he?"

"Yes, he did," the officer replied. "We told you to leave the Negro players at home. It's against the law for them and the whites to play on the same field." The officer looked over at Robinson, who had taken a seat on the bench. "Get him off the bench too. They can't sit together on the benches either. Tell him I said to go."

Hopper didn't want to disobey the officer. But he didn't want to embarrass Robinson by telling him to leave the bench. But as the small crowd hollered for the game to go on, Hopper walked toward the bench. The officer followed him the whole way.

Hopper began speaking slowly. "Ah, Jackie, the officer says … "

Robinson stopped him. "Okay, skipper," he said. Then he and Wright got up from the bench and headed for the clubhouse.

Normally, Branch Rickey would have spent most of his time in Florida watching the Brooklyn Dodgers prepare for their season. But this was not a normal spring training, not with his "noble experiment" of integration underway with the Royals. So Rickey spent a good part of the spring watching the Royals and cheering on Jackie Robinson. Whenever Robinson reached first base, Rickey would shout from the stands. "Be daring," he would say. "Take a bigger lead. Worry that pitcher into a sweat."

When Robinson hurt his arm, Rickey insisted that he learn how to play first base. At that position, he wouldn't have to throw as much as he did at shortstop. To Rickey, this seemed like the best way to keep Robinson playing and gaining valuable experience.

Although Rickey hadn't played baseball in decades, he took time to help Robinson learn his new position. Rickey was always ready to support Robinson. But he was careful to avoid making any promises about making the team. Still, Rickey tried to boost Robinson's spirits with a kind word here and there. He told Robinson, "We know you're going to make a great success."

Before the end of spring training, Rickey signed two more black players: pitcher Don Newcombe and catcher Roy Campanella. He knew some players and reporters still questioned if any blacks were good enough for the Majors. But he was sure he was right to try to integrate baseball. Even while some opponents of integration attacked him, Rickey was determined to make sure the color line was broken forever.

A YEAR IN MONTREAL

3

With spring training over, the Montreal Royals were ready to start their season against the Jersey City Giants. Branch Rickey made the short trip from Brooklyn to New Jersey to watch. Both Jackie Robinson and Johnny Wright had made the team. Robinson was in the starting lineup, playing second base.

Before the game, Frank Shaughnessy approached Rickey. Shaughnessy was the president of the International League, which included the Royals. Rickey and Shaughnessy had known each other since the 1920s, and Rickey considered him a friend. Now Shaughnessy asked Rickey to reconsider letting Robinson play when the team traveled to Baltimore. The Royals were scheduled to play there in 10 days.

Most International League teams were based in or near New York State. Rickey had hoped that this region would be more welcoming of the newly integrated Royals than Florida had been. The Baltimore Orioles, though, bordered the South. Based in Maryland, the Orioles were the top farm team of the Cleveland Indians. During the Civil War, Maryland had been one of only four states with slavery that did not join the South to fight the North. But racism lingered in parts of the state, especially in Baltimore.

"The people are up in arms in Baltimore," Shaughnessy said. "There could be rioting in the streets if Robinson plays there."

Rickey told Shaughnessy that he didn't expect that much trouble. "Anyhow," he said, "the time has come for us to give democracy a chance. We solve nothing by backing away — in fact, we'll encourage every agitator in Maryland if we show fear. Robinson is part of the Royals. He will play wherever the team plays."

Jackie Robinson

Jersey City, New Jersey, April 18, 1946

At the Jersey City ballpark on opening day, Jackie Robinson saw that Clay Hopper had placed him at second base. Before the game, a brass band played "The Star Spangled Banner." As he listened to the music, Robinson's heart thumped wildly. He could feel his stomach rumble with nerves. The stadium was packed, with more people in the stands than there were seats. Many of the fans were black.

Robinson's stomach was doing flip flops and his knees felt weak when he came up for his first at bat. He hit a soft ground ball and was easily thrown out. The next time he came to bat, two of his teammates were on base. Robinson swung and felt his bat make solid contact. He watched as the ball sailed over the left field fence for a home run. As Robinson trotted past third base, Clay Hopper gave him a pat on the back. In the dugout, his teammates joined in the celebration.

When the game was over, Robinson had collected four hits, scored four runs, and stolen two bases. All afternoon, Robinson had heard the crowd applaud his fine play. When the game was over, many of the fans, both black and white, mobbed him. They shouted their congratulations as he made his way off the field. Robinson felt good as he left the stadium. He felt that as long as he tried hard and played well, white fans would accept him. And if the fans supported him, surely he had a good chance to succeed.

Rachel Robinson
Baltimore, Maryland, April 1946

Rachel Robinson traveled with the Royals as they made their first road trip before going to Montreal. Jack got off to a decent start, with 12 hits and six stolen bases in his first eight games. Then, on April 27, she sat behind the Royals bench as Jack played his first game against the Baltimore Orioles.

Cold weather kept attendance down — Rachel could see the stadium was less than half full. But many in the crowd were quick to show their anger about a black man playing with whites.

As soon as Jack took the field, a white man near Rachel began shouting racist taunts. He encouraged others around him to join in. As the game went on, the crowd became increasingly vicious and hateful. Rachel began to fear that Jack might even be physically attacked.

Segregation of public facilities continued to be common in Baltimore, Maryland, during the 1940s.

Jack managed just one hit during the game, which the Royals lost. Afterward, Rachel sat with him in their hotel room and cried.

"I don't know if this it worth it, Jack," she said. "What good is breaking the color barrier if something happens to you?"

"I'll be fine," he replied. "I know it's hard on you. It's hard on me too, to keep my mouth shut and not defend myself. But it will get better."

Rachel returned to the park the next day. The Royals were playing a doubleheader. The temperature was in the mid 60s, and this time the stadium was filled. There were also clearly more black fans at today's game, though they were forced to sit in segregated areas.

The Royals lost the first game that day, and Jack again struggled at the plate, getting just one hit. But in the second game, he had three hits and scored four runs in the Royals' 10–0 victory.

After the game, Jack said, "It means so much to me to hear all the black fans cheering when I do well."

"I know, Jack," Rachel said. "Me too."

After the Baltimore series, the Royals finally headed to Montreal. Although Jackie Robinson had visited Montreal the previous October, now it would be home.

Canada had a small black population, compared to the United States. Slavery had once been legal there, but it was outlawed in Canada almost 30 years before the U.S. Civil War. In Montreal, at least, most people did not show the prejudice against blacks that was so common in the United States. The attitude Robinson experienced from fans and journalists felt very different than what he'd known in the United States. People on the street smiled at Robinson, and some even stopped to shake his hand.

Some of his Southern teammates, Robinson sensed, were still uneasy playing with him. But he was determined to keep showing his talents with his bat and glove. He hoped that if he did that, all of his teammates would support him.

Rachel Robinson

For the first month they were in Montreal, Rachel Robinson and Jack lived in a guest house. Then Rachel began to hunt for an apartment, a place they could really call home. She found a nice place in a largely French-speaking neighborhood. When she wasn't at the ballpark watching Jack play, Rachel often made clothes for herself and the baby. In June she finally told Jack she was pregnant. He was thrilled at the news.

It didn't take long for the Robinsons to make friends in Montreal. As her pregnancy progressed, Rachel got support and advice from some of the women in the neighborhood. She and Jack became friends with the couple next door. They became even closer to Sam and Belle Maltin. Sam was a white sports journalist who wrote about the Royals for a Montreal newspaper. He supported the integration of baseball. Rachel enjoyed it when the Maltins took them to concerts or invited them to dinner.

Belle knitted Rachel a sweater, and it became one of her favorite pieces of clothing.

Rachel saw Jack achieve more success on the field. His batting average was consistently well over .300 — the sign of an excellent hitter. Although the fans were friendly in Montreal, Jack still faced racism when the team traveled. When he told her about the taunts from opposing players, she tried to comfort him.

Rachel wanted to help Jack relax and stay focused on playing well. Because of this, she decided to keep another secret from him. At times, she developed a high fever and her doctor couldn't explain why. When the Royals traveled and Jack called home, he would ask how she was. "Everything's just fine," she would reply. But Rachel always felt better when the team came back to Montreal.

Jackie Robinson

Montreal, Canada, August 1946

Going into August, Jackie Robinson continued to hit at a hot pace. His batting average rose over .370 at times, good enough to lead the league.

The Royals were playing well as a team too. It began to look likely that they would end the regular season with the best record in the International League.

Despite his success on the field, Robinson continued to feel stress. He continued to hear the occasional taunts from fans and players. And Rachel's pregnancy was another concern. He told the Royals' business manager Mel Jones, "No one knows what I'm going through."

All of this stress took a toll on Robinson. He had trouble sleeping at times, and he lost his appetite. A doctor told him he needed rest and that he should take off at least five days. But he could only bring himself to miss three games. When the doctor told him he wasn't physically sick, Robinson was able to relax. His nerves improved and he was eager to play again.

The regular season ended on September 8. Robinson's average had fallen from its peak but he still finished as the best hitter in the league. He also led the league in runs scored and finished second in stolen bases.

The Royals then entered the playoffs, beating the Newark Bears and the Syracuse Chiefs. Next, the Royals would have to face the Louisville Colonels in the Little World Series. The winner of the best-of-seven-game series would be crowned the top minor-league team.

The Royals played the first three games in Louisville, Kentucky. Racism was strong there. The Colonels limited the number of black fans, so the stands were filled with mostly white people. As the series began, Robinson heard some of the worst taunts he had experienced all year. His play fell off, and the Royals won just one of the three games in Louisville.

The series then moved to Montreal, and Robinson excelled once again. Game four was tied after nine innings, so the play went into extra innings. Robinson got a walk-off hit in the bottom of the tenth to win the game for the Royals. He had three hits in game five, which the Royals won 5–3. In game six, Robinson had two hits and scored a run. The Royals won the championship with a 2–0 victory.

Clay Hopper

As the last game of the Little World Series ended, happy Royals fans stormed the field to celebrate. Clay Hopper joined his team in the clubhouse, where they could hear the shouting fans. The fans were refusing to leave the park until Jackie Robinson came out. He had hit .400 for the series and made several spectacular fielding plays. The fans knew Robinson was the hero for the season.

Hopper went back out into the stadium. Some of the fans lifted him onto their shoulders and paraded him around the field. When they set him down, the fans then gave the same hero's treatment to pitcher Curt Davis. But it was Robinson they really wanted, and he finally stepped out to join the crowd.

When the celebration ended, Robinson returned to the clubhouse. Hopper went over to him and stuck out his hand to shake Robinson's.

"Jackie, you're a real ballplayer and a gentleman," he said. "It's been wonderful having you on the team."

"Thanks, Skipper," Robinson said. "It's been wonderful playing under you."

Hopper then left the clubhouse to head back home to Mississippi.

Clay Hopper (left) and Jackie Robinson (right) say goodbye after the Little World Series of 1946.

GOING TO BROOKLYN

4

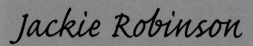

Jackie Robinson

Havana, Cuba, February 1947

Before the 1947 season, both the Royals and the Brooklyn Dodgers traveled to Havana, Cuba, for spring training. While Jackie Robinson went to Cuba, Rachel stayed in California with their infant son. Jackie Robinson Jr. had been born on November 18, 1946.

Before Robinson left California, Rachel warned him to watch his temper. Robinson agreed with her. While he didn't think he was a hothead, he could get angry when he was treated unfairly. He knew he would have to restrain his anger at times. He didn't want to embarrass himself or his team.

Despite his great season with the Royals, Robinson still was not guaranteed a spot on the Dodgers.

And once again, he was not allowed to stay with the white players during training. He and three other black players stayed at a separate hotel 15 miles from the training camp. Robinson was unhappy about being segregated from the team. But he accepted it because Branch Rickey had arranged it. He knew Rickey wanted to lower the risk of any kind of racial incident in Havana.

Robinson also wasn't happy when Mel Jones of the Royals told him to practice playing first base. Robinson wanted to play second, where he had done well the year before. But he did as he was told.

Dixie Walker
Havana, Cuba, March 1947

Dixie Walker was not happy when he arrived in Cuba for spring training. A star outfielder for the Dodgers, Walker lived in Birmingham, Alabama. He had no desire to play with Jackie Robinson or any other black man. He thought about his business back in his hometown. He knew his customers would not approve of his playing on an integrated team.

As the Dodgers and Royals prepared to play several training games in Panama, Walker decided to take action. He recruited four other players, all but one from the South, to sign a petition. In it, they told Branch Rickey they wouldn't play for the Dodgers if Robinson was on the team.

Walker's roommate was backup catcher Bobby Bragan. Bragan, a Southerner, also signed the petition. He told Walker, "I grew up segregated. That's what I'm used to and how I want to play ball."

Jackie Robinson (left) tags a base runner during spring training in Havana, Cuba.

Walker and the others who backed the petition approached several other Southern players to see if they would sign it. Outfielder Pete Reiser, who had been born in Missouri, said no. Reiser said a black doctor had taken care of his daughter when he was sick. "If I would trust her life to a black man," Reiser said, "why wouldn't I play baseball with one?"

Next, Walker approached shortstop Pee Wee Reese. One of baseball's best shortstops and the leader of the team, Reese was from Kentucky. He considered signing the petition, then said no. "Robinson has a right to be here, if he's good enough," Reese said.

Branch Rickey
Brooklyn, New York, March 1947

While his top two teams went to Panama, Branch Rickey remained in Brooklyn. One day, he got a call from Harold Parrott, the Dodgers' traveling secretary. One of Parrott's jobs was to make arrangements for the team on road trips.

Parrott recounted a conversation with Kirby Higbe, one of the team's best pitchers. Higbe had signed a petition against Robinson, and told Parrott about it.

Rickey realized that a revolt might be brewing in Panama. He worried that if this continued to grow it could ruin his noble experiment. In light of this, he took a plane to Panama right away. When he arrived, he made plans to bring in four of the players closely linked to the petition. He would meet with Higbe, outfielder Carl Furillo, Bobby Bragan, and pitcher Hugh Casey one by one. Rickey knew Dixie Walker was linked to the petition, but he had left Panama to deal with a family emergency.

Talking to the players, Rickey stressed that Robinson could help the team. He also told each man that he didn't expect them to be friendly to Robinson off the field. But if they couldn't accept him as a teammate, Rickey would be glad to trade them.

Furillo, the one Northerner involved, quickly backed down and apologized. Casey also changed his mind quickly. But Higbe and Bragan still resisted Rickey's efforts to integrate the team. Bragan said he was not part of the petition effort, but he admitted he had strong feeling about integration. "I'm from Texas, Mr. Rickey," he said. "My friends there would never forgive me."

"You and nobody else is going to tell me who to play on this team," Rickey said. "Do you want to play with Robinson?"

"No, I do not!" Bragan replied. "I'd rather be traded than play with him."

"Then I may accommodate you, sir!" Rickey said. He paused for a moment, then added, "but I must say, I do appreciate your honesty."

The heated exchange left Rickey shaking.

Jackie Robinson
Balboa, Panama, March 1947

Jackie Robinson was preparing for the upcoming exhibition games against the Dodgers when Branch Rickey called. He asked Robinson to meet him over at his hotel.

"Nothing you did last year at Montreal means a thing," Rickey said when Robinson arrived.

"This is where you will have to make the grade. I want the Dodger players to see how good you are and how much you can help the team. After all, these boys are thinking about winning the National League pennant."

At the ballpark that day, Robinson got two hits and played well in the field. As the series between the two clubs went on, Robinson continued his fine play. He ended up with the highest batting average between the two teams and stole seven bases. He didn't know if he had played as well as Rickey had hoped he would. But he hoped he had shown that he was ready for the Majors.

Wendell Smith

Havana, Cuba, March 1947

After the Panama series, the Dodgers and the Royals returned to Cuba. Wendell Smith met with Branch Rickey in the president's hotel room.

"It's going to happen," Rickey told him. "On April 10, we're going to give Robinson a contract to play for the Dodgers."

When the conversation ended, Smith ran to Robinson's room, bubbling with excitement. He repeated the news Rickey had just told him.

"If Mr. Rickey was going to put me on the Dodgers, he'd have put me on the club by now," Robinson said, laughing. "Didn't I prove down in Panama that I could hit big league pitching and steal against big league catchers?"

Smith didn't say anything more. But on March 29, he wrote a new story for the *Pittsburgh Courier*. He included the news Rickey had given him: Robinson would play in Brooklyn in 1947.

Jackie Robinson

Brooklyn, New York, April 10, 1947

Jackie Robinson and the Montreal Royals were about to play their last exhibition game against the Dodgers in Brooklyn. Robinson got a call that morning. A staff member at Branch Rickey's office told him to come there before the game.

Rickey gave Robinson the news when he arrived: He would be promoted to the Dodgers.

Robinson played for the Royals that day as planned. In the sixth inning, after he grounded into a double play, Robinson's teammates began to congratulate him. They had just learned he would be playing in Brooklyn. Robinson simply smiled from ear to ear.

Jackie Robinson receives a warm welcome from fans of the Dodgers on April 10, 1947.

OPENING DAY
AND BEYOND

5

Jackie and Rachel Robinson with their son, Jackie Jr.

Rachel Robinson

With the good news that Jack had made the team, Rachel and four-month-old Jackie Jr. came to join him. At first the family stayed in a hotel in the center of Manhattan. They had just one room, but that suited Rachel for the time being. Housing was tough to find in New York. But Rachel planned to hunt for their own apartment soon.

Rachel spent most days caring for their baby in the hotel. Reporters sometimes stopped by, hoping to interview Jackie. Because they couldn't cook in the room, Rachel and Jack took turns going to a nearby cafeteria to get food. Life was challenging for Rachel. She had to take care of her child while worrying about her husband and what the future would bring.

The Dodgers' first game of the season was April 15. While Jack headed off to Ebbets Field in Brooklyn, Rachel got Jackie Jr. ready. The spring day was chilly and Jackie Jr. was fighting an illness.

She dressed her son in a new spring outfit, then headed down to the streets, feeling nervous. She realized that she didn't even know how to get to the ballpark. She didn't want to use the subway because she was afraid she'd get lost. Several cab drivers refused to make the trip to Ebbets Field. They didn't want to leave Manhattan to go all the way to Brooklyn. But Rachel kept hailing cabs. She was not going to miss Jack's historic moment.

Joel Oppenheimer

Manhattan, New York, April 15, 1947

Home on a break from college, 18-year-old Joel Oppenheimer was helping out in his father's leather-goods store in Manhattan. Oppenheimer was sweeping the floor when his dad approached him.

"If you could do anything in the world today, what would you like to do?" his father asked. Oppenheimer struggled to answer, so finally his father said, "Wouldn't you like to be at Ebbets Field today?"

Oppenheimer was a big baseball fan and he knew that Jackie Robinson was making his Major League debut that day. He was shocked, though, that his father knew who Robinson was, and that Oppenheimer would want to see the game. He put down his broom and headed for Ebbets Field.

Oppenheimer knew about some of the talented black players who played well against white teams in exhibition games. But Robinson's playing for the Dodgers was completely different. He represented all the black players who had been denied a chance to play in the Majors. And with Robinson's talent, he just might help Brooklyn win the World Series.

At the park, Oppenheimer had to stand with other fans behind third base. Most of the people around him were black. Oppenheimer realized that, for the first time in his life, he was surrounded by people of another race.

Jackie Robinson

Brooklyn, New York, April 15, 1947

Wearing number 42 on his jersey, Jackie Robinson came out of the Dodgers dugout and took his position

Opening day at Ebbets Field in Brooklyn, New York, April 15, 1947

at first base. Somewhere out there Rachel was in the stands watching. So were thousands of black people who wanted to see him succeed. Last night he had thanked God for the opportunities he had earned. Now he tried to just focus and not think about the importance of the game.

The Dodgers were playing the Boston Braves, and Robinson got involved right away. The first Braves batter hit a ground ball to third baseman Spider Jorgensen, who collected the ball and threw it to Robinson for the out at first. It was an easy play, but the crowd roared.

His first time at the plate, Robinson faced Johnny Sain, one of the best pitchers in the Majors. Robinson grounded out to third. In his next at bat, he flied out to left. He realized that getting hits against the best Major League pitchers was not going to be easy.

Joel Oppenheimer

Brooklyn, New York, April 15, 1947

Joel Oppenheimer watched Jackie Robinson struggle at the plate. But his fielding was sharp.

After one particularly good play, the black fans around Oppenheimer showed their appreciation. "Jackie, Jackie, Jackie," they yelled. Oppenheimer joined in too.

Oppenheimer then heard someone behind him yelling, "Yonkel, Yonkel, Yonkel." As a Jewish man, Oppenheimer recognized this as Yiddish, a language many Jewish immigrants spoke. *Yonkel* meant "Jackie." Oppenheimer turned around to see a small Jewish man showing his support for Robinson. The man and Oppenheimer were the only whites in that part of the crowd. Oppenheimer was impressed that they had all come together to support Robinson.

Jackie Robinson
Brooklyn, New York, April 1947

Despite a tough start at the plate, Jackie Robinson felt good about his first Major League game. He finally reached base on an error and scored as the Dodgers went on to win 5–3.

Later, back at his hotel, a reporter stopped by. "I was comfortable on that field," Robinson told him.

"The Brooklyn players have been swell and they were encouraging all the way. The Brooklyn crowd was certainly on my side, but I don't know how it will be in other parks."

The Dodgers' first road game was still in New York, against the New York Giants. On a Friday afternoon, with the stadium packed with fans, Robinson came to the plate in the third inning. He hit a fastball and watched it sail over the left field fence and bounce off the scoreboard. It was his first Major League home run. Robinson felt good as he rounded the bases. As he crossed the plate, Robinson's teammate Tommy Tatum shook his hand. Despite the homer, Robinson was disappointed that the Dodgers lost the game. They lost the next one too, but Robinson had gotten five hits in the series.

Jackie Robinson (right) and Tommy Tatum (left) shake hands as Robinson crosses the plate after hitting his first home run as a Dodger.

Snow caused the team's next two games in Boston to be cancelled. The Dodgers then headed home to play three games with the Philadelphia Phillies. Philadelphia's manager, Ben Chapman, was known as a ferocious "bench jockey." He liked to bully opposing players from the dugout. His players were just as bad. Robinson wondered if there might be trouble in this series.

Ben Chapman

Brooklyn, New York, April 22, 1947

From his playing days to now, Philadelphia Phillies manager Ben Chapman liked to taunt opposing players. He wasn't the only one to do it, of course. Bench jockeying had been part of baseball for a long time. As far as Chapman was concerned, an opponent's ethnicity was fair game. He remembered the taunts directed at him when he was a rookie: "Hey, you redneck so-and-so, go back to Alabama where you belong." But the Tennessee-born Chapman was especially upset when Jackie Robinson joined the Dodgers. He strongly opposed integrating baseball.

As Robinson stepped up to the plate for the first time against the Phillies, Chapman led the jeering. Soon he and his players were calling Robinson every racial slur they could think of. They told Robinson to go back to the jungle and that he wasn't wanted in the Majors. They suggested he would pass on diseases to the other Dodger players if they touched his towels or combs. Chapman and his players didn't stop their insults as the series went on.

Eddie Stanky

Brooklyn, New York, April 23, 1947

The fans in Brooklyn called Eddie Stanky "the Brat," but he knew the nickname was a compliment. It reflected his fiery spirit on the field, his intense desire to win at all costs. Stanky was not put off by Jackie Robinson's race. If he could help the Dodgers win, Stanky was all for Branch Rickey's noble experiment. On opening day, when the Dodgers' infielders posed for a picture, Stanky put his arm on Robinson's shoulder.

Now, as the Phillies series went on for a second day, the constant taunting of Robinson made Stanky angry. Bench jockeying might be part of the game, but Ben Chapman and the others were going too far. He also knew that Robinson could not respond in any way. During the second game of the series, Stanky couldn't take it anymore. He shouted to the Phillies' bench, "Listen, you yellow-bellied coward, why don't you yell at someone who can answer back?"

The Dodgers' infielders (from left) Spider Jorgensen, Pee Wee Reese, Eddie Stanky, and Jackie Robinson pose together on opening day.

Jackie Robinson

Brooklyn, New York, April 1947

Playing against the Phillies, Jackie Robinson heard a level of hatred he had never experienced before on the ball field. Adding to his frustration, he knew Branch Rickey expected him to take the abuse and not answer back. Robinson imagined throwing down his bat, going over to the Phillies' bench, and punching one of the white players. But he didn't do that. Instead, he gritted his teeth and just went on with the game.

GOING TO THE WORLD SERIES

6

Rachel Robinson

As the season went on, Rachel Robinson watched as Jack's confidence grew. His batting average went up, and by mid-June it was close to .300. But she still worried, knowing the tremendous strain he was under because of the racism that swirled around him.

Racism sometimes came into their tiny Brooklyn apartment too. Rachel opened up more than one letter sent to their home that contained a death threat against Jack. She made a point of going to every Dodgers home game, to show Jack her support and love. After games, Jack would sometimes pour out his anger and frustration over a racist remark or his own bad play. But when he did well, Rachel shared with him the joy of his success.

Rachel also began to spend time with the other players' wives. At first she was usually alone as she waited for Jack to leave the clubhouse after a game. But one day, Norma King, the wife of pitcher Clyde King, approached Rachel. Norma had seen Rachel standing by herself outside Ebbets Field. Norma told her that the other wives waited for their husbands in a walkway under the stands. "You belong in here with us," Norma told Rachel.

Slowly Rachel became friendly with some of the women, particularly Joan Hodges, wife of catcher Gil Hodges. Talking to a reporter that season, Rachel said, "When they gossip I join right in and gossip with them." Still, Rachel knew the white wives were closer to each other than she was with them.

At times, Rachel went on the road with Jack. On these trips she had to sit in the stands and listen to the taunts aimed at her husband. But in Brooklyn, she always felt comfortable and at home.

Jackie Robinson

Brooklyn, New York, August 1947

Despite the racism he faced, Robinson kept playing hard. By August his average remained near .300. On the Dodgers he felt accepted as a key part of the team. But some opposing players still resented his presence in the Majors. In mid-August, the Dodgers were playing the St. Louis Cardinals in Brooklyn. The Dodgers had once had a big lead in the pennant race, but the Cardinals had closed the gap. Robinson knew that some of the Cardinals players didn't like him. He had read the reports that some of them wanted to go on strike rather than play against him.

It didn't take long for the August series against the Cardinals to get ugly. It started when Cardinals outfielder Enos "Country" Slaughter hit a ball to Robinson at first base. Robinson made the stop, then tagged the bag. But while his foot was still on the base, Slaughter drove his spiked cleats into Robinson's lower calf. Robinson clutched his leg as the pain hit him. The location was too high for this to have been an accident. He saw some of his teammates charge out of the dugout to protest the play.

Despite the injury, which left bruises on his leg, Robinson finished the game. The Dodgers lost. In the clubhouse, he watched Dodgers trainer Doc Wender treat the injury. "You were lucky," Wender said. "This could have been much more serious."

Later, speaking to reporters, Robinson let them know he thought Slaughter had spiked him on purpose. "What else could it have been?" he asked the reporters.

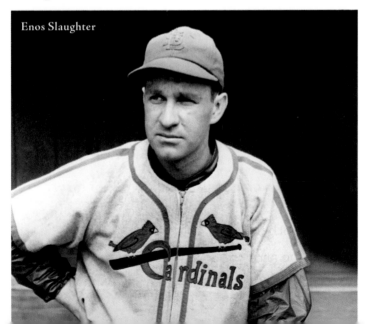

Enos Slaughter

Branch Rickey

All season, Branch Rickey had watched Jackie Robinson keep his temper, as he had promised. He had also excelled on the field. The Dodgers had been good the year before, finishing second in the National League. But Rickey knew Robinson had made the team better.

Robinson had also helped draw huge crowds to Ebbets Field. He had even helped draw big crowds to other teams' parks. Both black and white baseball fans wanted to see him play.

In September, with the season coming to a close, the Dodgers were solidly in first place. Rickey agreed to requests by some people in the community to hold a special day to honor Robinson's accomplishments. They planned the celebration for September 23.

Without telling Robinson, Rickey arranged for his mother to fly to Brooklyn for the occasion. When she arrived, Mallie Robinson thanked

Rickey for giving her son a chance to play in the Major Leagues. "Don't thank me, Mrs. Robinson," Rickey said. "I have to thank you. If it hadn't been for you, there wouldn't be any Jackie."

The night before the celebration, the Dodgers clinched the pennant. Rickey told reporters, "I'm pleased with everything in the world tonight." But he reminded everyone that the Dodgers were not finished: "We have to keep our minds on our next job — the World Series."

On September 23, Rickey watched a crowd jam into Ebbets Field for the celebration. They saw Robinson receive many gifts, including a new car and a gold watch. In his brief comments, Robinson thanked many people, including his teammates, for helping him to improve his game.

Later, Rickey saw a group of women going through the stands. They were collecting signatures for a petition asking Congress to make lynching a federal crime. As Rickey had hoped, his noble experiment was about more than simply letting black people play in the Major Leagues.

For Jackie Robinson, the day in his honor was just the first of many tributes he received. The *Sporting News*, a national sports newspaper, gave baseball's first ever Rookie of the Year Award to Robinson. He also saw his face on the cover of *Time* magazine. He ended the season hitting .297. He was second in the Majors in runs scored with 125. He led the league in stolen bases with 29.

Robinson had started the season a lonely man, out to achieve what many people thought was impossible. But as the regular season ended, he felt part of the team. And he had shown that his skills, not his skin color, mattered most on the field. Off the field, he and Rachel now felt more included too. The other Dodgers and their wives invited them to several parties before the World Series.

The World Series started on September 30. The Dodgers were facing the New York Yankees at their field in the Bronx, New York. The Yankees had a long tradition of great players and great teams. Most sportswriters gave the Dodgers little chance of winning. For Robinson, it was simply a thrill to be playing in the World Series in his first year in the Majors.

When he spoke to a crowd of Dodgers fans before the Series, he wanted to show his confidence. With a smile he said, "We will beat the Yankees." But Robinson read the newspapers. He saw what the sportswriters were saying and realized his team would be the underdogs this time.

Yogi Berra
The Bronx, New York, September 30, 1947

Yankees catcher Yogi Berra had seen Jackie Robinson's success in the 1947 season. But he wasn't particularly worried about Robinson, and he knew the same went for his teammates. Before the first game, Berra told reporters that he had played against

Robinson the year before in the International League. "Robinson never stole a base against me," he said. "We know all about him. We know when he's going to run and when he's going to bunt."

In the first inning, Berra took his position behind home plate as Robinson came up for the first time. Yankee pitcher Frank Shea threw carefully to him, but Robinson earned a walk. On the second pitch to the next batter, Berra saw Robinson sprint for second base. The catcher came out of his crouch throwing. He watched the ball sail across the infield and bounce about 2 feet short into shortstop Phil Rizzuto's glove. He tagged Robinson, but it was too late — he was safe.

Jackie Robinson (center) safely steals second base during the 1947 World Series.

Jackie Robinson

Jackie Robinson felt good after stealing his first base of the World Series. He beat Yogi Berra's throw and made it to second base. Soon after that, he got caught in a rundown between second and third base. He zigged and zagged on the basepath long enough for his teammate Pete Reiser to reach second base. Later that inning Reiser scored the game's first run. But it was a difficult game for Brooklyn, and a difficult series. The Dodgers lost the first two games in the Bronx.

Robinson was in good spirits, though, when the series moved to Ebbets Field. He figured the Dodgers had a much better chance playing in their own ballpark. They won two out of three there before the series moved back to Yankee Stadium.

Then the Dodgers won game six to tie the series at 3–3. Outfielder Al Gionfriddo ensured the win with a long running catch off the bat of Yankee superstar Joe DiMaggio. Robinson thought it was one of the best catches he'd ever seen.

Jackie Robinson at Ebbets Field in Brooklyn, New York, 1947

In the end the Yankees won Game Seven to become baseball's champions. Robinson thought he had played solidly, but not spectacularly. In the clubhouse after the final game, he felt bad about losing the series. But he had no regrets about the season. Branch Rickey came in to speak to the team and told them how proud he was of them. Then, reporters poured into the clubhouse, and some headed for Robinson. Sitting on a stool with a baseball in his hand, he said simply, "We lost. We'll get them next year."

After he changed out of his uniform, Robinson shook hands with his teammates. It made him feel good to hear some of them say how well he played all season. It had been a difficult year, but Robinson felt he had carried out the noble experiment with dignity.

"We lost. We'll get them next year."

EPILOGUE

Jackie Robinson went on to play nine more seasons with the Brooklyn Dodgers. In 1955, he helped them win their first World Series, after once again playing the Yankees. By that year, the Dodgers had several other black stars, and most other Major League teams had signed black players as well.

During his career, Robinson won the National League's Most Valuable Player Award in 1949, when he led the league in hitting. He played in six All-Star Games, and in 1962 he was elected to the National Baseball Hall of Fame.

After leaving baseball, Robinson spent time working to improve the rights of all African-Americans. In 1972 he wrote that he couldn't "rejoice in the good things I've been permitted to work for and learn while the humblest of my brothers is down deep in a hole hollering for help and not being heard."

Robinson died the year he wrote those words. At 52, he suffered a heart attack in his home. After his death, *The New York Times* said that his breaking the color line had a huge impact on American society. That made Robinson, the paper said, "perhaps America's most significant athlete."

Seven years earlier, Branch Rickey had also died of a heart attack. After making history by integrating baseball, Rickey left the Dodgers in 1950. He sold

Jackie and Rachel Robinson joined the March on Washington for Jobs and Freedom on August 28, 1963.

his share of the team and took a job running the Pittsburgh Pirates until 1959. For a time, he also tried to organize a new major baseball league. Rickey finished his career in baseball working for the St. Louis Cardinals. He was elected to the National Baseball Hall of Fame in 1967.

Roy Campanella joined Robinson and Rickey in the Hall of Fame in 1969. Playing with the Dodgers for 10 years, Campanella was chosen the Rookie of the Year in 1949 and the National League's Most Valuable Player in 1951, 1953, and 1955.

Of all the people who were close to Jackie Robinson in 1947, one was still alive as of 2017: his wife, Rachel. After Jackie's baseball career ended, she earned another degree in nursing and held important positions at several medical organizations. She also was active in charity, trying to help young people go to college. She did some of that work through an organization she founded and named for her husband.

In the decades after Jackie Robinson's death, both Major League Baseball and the country as a whole have honored him. In 1984 President Ronald Reagan awarded him the Medal of Freedom, the highest honor an American civilian can receive. In 1997 the government issued gold and silver coins to mark the 50th anniversary of Robinson's Major League debut. The same year, Major League Baseball announced that Robinson's number 42 would be retired by all teams. This meant that no other player would ever be given that number again.

In 1982 Jackie Robinson became the first Major League player to appear on a U.S. postage stamp.

TIMELINE

1884 Moses Fleetwood Walker plays for the Toledo Blue Stockings of the major league American Association

1890s The introduction of the color line keeps blacks from playing with whites in professional baseball

1919 Jackie Robinson is born on January 31

1939 Robinson begins his college career at UCLA

1942 Robinson is drafted into the U.S. Army

JULY 17, 1944 Robinson is arrested for refusing to move to the back of an Army bus

AUGUST 3, 1944 Robinson faces an Army court-martial but is acquitted at the trial

NOVEMBER 28, 1944 Robinson receives an honorable discharge from the Army

1944 Boston city councilman Isadore Muchnick insists that the Boston Red Sox hold tryouts for black players

1945 Robinson begins playing baseball for the Kansas City Monarchs of the Negro League

APRIL 16, 1945 Wendell Smith takes Robinson and two other black players to a tryout with the Boston Red Sox

AUGUST 1945 Clyde Sukeforth scouts Robinson for the Dodgers

OCTOBER 23, 1945 Robinson signs a contract with the Brooklyn Dodgers organization to play for the Montreal Royals of the International League

FEBRUARY 10, 1946 Robinson and Rachel Isum marry

MARCH 1946 Robinson begins spring training with the Royals

MARCH 17, 1946 Robinson makes his debut in organized professional baseball by playing in an exhibition game between the Royals and the Brooklyn Dodgers

APRIL 18, 1946 Robinson appears in his first regular-season game with the Royals and hits a home run

OCTOBER 1946 The Montreal Royals win the Little World Series

NOVEMBER 18, 1946 The Robinsons have their first child, Jackie Robinson Jr.

APRIL 15, 1947 Robinson makes his debut with the Dodgers in a game against the Boston Braves at Ebbets Field in Brooklyn. He becomes the first African-American to play in the Major Leagues in the modern era.

OCTOBER 1947 Robinson becomes baseball's first-ever Rookie of the Year

OCTOBER 1949 Robinson wins the National League's Most Valuable Player (MVP) award with a .342 batting average and 37 stolen bases

OCTOBER 4, 1955 Robinson helps the Dodgers win the team's first World Series

JANUARY 23, 1962 Robinson is elected to the National Baseball Hall of Fame

1967 Branch Rickey is elected to the National Baseball Hall of Fame

OCTOBER 23, 1972 Robinson dies of a heart attack at his home in Stamford, Connecticut

1984 President Ronald Reagan awards Robinson the Medal of Freedom

1997 For the 50th anniversary of Robinson's historic first season, Major League Baseball retires his number, 42

GLOSSARY

court-martial (KORT-MAR-shuhl)—trial used in the military

exhibition (ek-suh-BI-shuhn)—athletic event or game that does not count in league standings, often played before or after the regular season

integrate (IN-tuh-grate)—mix people from different races together

lynch (LYNCH)—to be put to death, often by hanging, by mob action and without legal authority

pennant (PEN-uhnt)—a triangular flag given to the best team in baseball's American and National Leagues; also, the championship itself

petition (puh-TISH-uhn)—a letter signed by many people asking leaders for a change

prejudice (PREJ-uh-diss)—the feeling that one group of people is less equal than another and does not deserve equal treatment

segregation (seg-ruh-GAY-shuhn)—the practice of keeping groups of people apart, especially based on race

CRITICAL THINKING QUESTIONS

1. Why did Branch Rickey want a player to break the color line?

2. Examine at least two examples of the racism Jackie Robinson faced while playing with the Royals or the Dodgers. How did he respond to these incidents?

3. Give one example of how Wendell Smith helped Robinson break the color line.

INTERNET SITES

Use FactHound to find Internet sites related to this book.

Visit *www.facthound.com*

Just type in 9781515779322 and go.

FURTHER READING

Hillstrom, Laurie Collier. *Jackie Robinson and the Integration of Baseball*. Detroit: Omnigraphics, Inc., 2013.

Muldoon, Kathleen M. *The Jim Crow Era*. North Mankato, Minn.: ABDO Publishing Company, 2014.

Peters, Gregory N. *The Negro Leagues*. North Mankato, Minn.: Capstone Press, 2014.

Robinson, Sharon. *The Hero Two Doors Down: Based on the True Story of Friendship Between a Boy and a Baseball Legend*. New York: Scholastic Press, 2016.

SELECTED BIBLIOGRAPHY

Campanella, Roy. *It's Good to Be Alive*. Lincoln, Nebr.: University of Nebraska Press, 1995.

Eig, Jonathan. *Opening Day: The Story of Jackie Robinson's First Season*. New York: Simon & Schuster, 2007.

Frommer, Harvey. *Rickey and Robinson: The Men Who Broke Baseball's Color Barrier*. Lanham, Md.: Taylor Trade Publishing, 1982.

Golenbock, Peter. *Bums: An Oral History of the Brooklyn Dodgers*. Mineola, N.Y.: Dover Publications, 2010.

Honig, Donald. *Baseball When the Grass Was Real: Baseball from the Twenties to the Forties Told by the Men Who Played It*. New York: Coward, McCann & Geoghegan, 1975.

Kahn, Roger. *Rickey & Robinson*. New York: Rodale, 2014.

Lamb, Chris. *Blackout: The Untold Story of Jackie Robinson's First Spring Training*. Lincoln, Nebr.: University of Nebraska Press, 2004.

Lowenfish, Lee. *Branch Rickey: Baseball's Ferocious Gentleman*. Lincoln, Nebr.: University of Nebraska Press, 2009.

Parrott, Harold. *The Lords of Baseball*. Atlanta: Longstreet Press, 2001.

Rampersad, Arnold. *Jackie Robinson: A Biography*. New York: Knopf, 1997.

Robinson, Jackie. *I Never Had It Made*. New York: G.P. Putnam's Sons, 1972.

Robinson, Rachel, and Lee Daniels. *Jackie Robinson: An Intimate Portrait*. New York: Harry N. Abrams, 1996.

Rowan, Carl, and Jackie Robinson. *Wait Till Next Year: The Story of Jackie Robinson*. New York: Random House, 1960.

Spatz, Lyle, ed. *The Team That Forever Changed Baseball and America: The 1947 Brooklyn Dodgers*. Lincoln, Nebr.: University of Nebraska Press and the Society for American Baseball Research, 2012.

Tygiel, Jules. *Baseball's Great Experiment: Jackie Robinson and His Legacy*. New York: Oxford University Press, 2008.

INDEX

ABOUT THE AUTHOR

Michael Burgan is a freelance writer who specializes in books for children and young adults, both fiction and nonfiction. A graduate of the University of Connecticut with a degree in history, Burgan is also a produced playwright and the editor of *The Biographer's Craft,* the newsletter for Biographers International Organization. He lives in Santa Fe, New Mexico.